I0026737

FIREFLY CULTURE

Praise for *Firefly Culture*

"Having spent most of my adult life working in corporate America, I have spent years focused on my income, my status and maintaining my position on the corporate ladder. Since beginning my journey to mindfulness and reading *Firefly Culture*, I have been able to change my focus.

"Using the practices learned in *Firefly Culture* and going back to the book when I get distracted, I feel I am on my way to being a more mindful, peaceful and compassionate person in all aspects of my life."
—FRANCINE LLERENA, Senior Mortgage Loan Officer
Rockledge, FL

"When I was employed by a company, I used to wish that my boss had been more understanding, fair and mindful of his employees. Now that I am the president of my own company and after reading Firefly Culture, I understand, practice and encourage mindfulness. This amazing book gave me the tools to implement mindfulness in the workplace. It has created a very positive work environment, improved well being, decreased stress levels and it has boosted productivity."
—INEVETT HAHN, President of
Hahn and Hahn Team, Inc., Winter Park, FL

"This was a very interesting read! I love all the positive ideas at the workplace. That is so needed in most every job I know of, especially ours!"
—KIM JACKSON AND KAREN DELEO, Owners of
The Title Station, Melbourne, FL

"From *Hippiebanker* to *Firefly Culture*, Camille has taken mindfulness to an entirely different level. Working in the corporate world, maintaining and managing sales plans and employees, all while having a balanced personal life can be hard to conquer. However, *Firefly Culture* is a reminder and way to grow and heal, personally and professionally. Bravo!"

—Josh Wendt, Sales & Education Market Manager
Estèe Lauder, Orlando, FL

"A wonderful book that gives us the tools to live a reflective and productive life. Very interesting and enlightening read. "

—Tina Galvin, Electrical Designer
Sparta, NJ

FIREFLY CULTURE

Illuminate Your Workplace
by Tuning In to

Mindfulness

Camille Sacco
Jasmine Alam Ph.D.

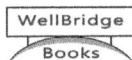

WellBridge
Books

WELLBRIDGE BOOKS
PORTLAND • OREGON • USA

WellBridge Books
An imprint of Six Degrees Publishing Group

Copyright © 2020
Camille Sacco and Jasmine Alam

All rights reserved under United States, International and Pan-American Copyright Conventions. No part of this book may be reproduced, distributed or transmitted in any form or by any means without the prior written consent of the copyright owner and the publisher, excepting brief quotes used in reviews. For information/inquiries please contact the publisher: Permissions@WellBridgebooks.com

ISBN: 978-1-942497-48-6
eISBN: 978-1-942497-49-3

U.S. Library of Congress Control Number 2020932755

Published in the United States of America
Front Cover Art by Harrison Lemire

The Authors and Publisher wish to thank Dave Potter for his generosity in granting permissions to use and reprint the meditation materials used in this book, which are also currently available at: palousemindfulness.com. Additional audio recordings are also available at www.camillesacco.com/meditations.

Disclaimer: This publication is designed as a source of information only and is not intended as a substitute for psychological treatment or professional services of any kind. The author and the publisher expressly disclaim responsibility for any adverse effects arising from the use or application of the information contained herein. If mental health treatment is required, readers should seek individual help and services from a licensed mental health professional.

Printed simultaneously in the United States of America
The United Kingdom and Australia

1 3 5 7 9 10 8 6 4 2

Contents

Preface

I DON'T KNOW ABOUT YOU, but one of the most memorable moments of my childhood is sitting on the front stoop of my house on a warm summer night watching fireflies. The neighborhood children would gather on our front lawn at dusk waiting patiently for that first glimpse of light. We would watch these beautiful creatures dancing in the night sky, lighting up from within, lights flashing on and off, trying to see if we could anticipate where they would light up next. At times, we would try and catch the fireflies, in a way, attempting to capture that source that allows them to illuminate from within. Where does it come from? What makes them glow? It all seemed so magical to me.

Looking back, I cherish those memories because they remind me of the freedom of youth—the carefree attitude of long summer nights, no responsibility and really being and living in the moment. Not worrying about yesterday, not stressing about tomorrow, but truly enjoying and living life in the present moment. As we get older, the joy of being present is lost and replaced with never ending TO DO lists that come with the responsibility of being an adult. Parenting, relationships and work take precedence over our lives. Hopefully, for most of us, our home life is dedicated to building a happy home, strong relationships, growing our soul and cultivating a strong sense of self. We strive to become better versions of ourselves. At home, it's important that we read self-help books, work on our inner life, strengthen our relationships, take care of our children, go to the gym or practice yoga, etc. We are encouraged to bring emotions such as love, compassion, empathy, patience and gratitude to our home life and to our relationships. Our well-being is a top priority. If you think about it, in our personal lives we are all attempting to be like fireflies, lighting up from within and shining our light on everyone we meet. We feel comfortable in doing this and actually strive to be like a firefly at home and in our relationships. We adopt a *Firefly Culture*, if you will, in our personal lives.

However, when we get to work and step through that front door, all that changes. Our culture at home does not mirror our culture at work. At work, it's ingrained in us to hide our emotions, to dim our light and just do the task at hand. Put our heads down and plow through the workday. At times, it seems easier to just drink the Kool-Aid, collect our paycheck at the end of the week, and call it a day. Then, on the weekends, we can go back to cultivating a life that we are truly proud of—a life that allows us to shine from within. But what if we decided to bring our inner light to work? To shine in the midst of darkness? To transform our culture at work into a Firefly Culture? A culture where we are not afraid to bring love, compassion, empathy, patience and gratitude to our coworkers, our employees, and our clients. Do you think it might make for a more meaningful and productive work life, both for ourselves and the people around us? So the question becomes . . . if this is so, how exactly do we integrate this Firefly Culture into our work lives? How do we drive the business, meet our sales goals, focus on giving great customer service, empower and motivate our employees AND remain rooted in the present moment, proudly shining our inner light?

It starts with a concept called *Mindfulness*. Mindfulness at its core simply means to be present, aware and not lost in thought. Recently, Harvard researchers have concluded that we are lost in thought almost 47% of the time.[1] That's almost half our waking existence! This is by no means insignificant and a practice to reduce this percentage must be top priority if we are to excel and thrive in all aspects of our lives. We can do this with a commitment to a consistent mindfulness practice.

To be perfectly clear, mindfulness is not something we have to attain or try to achieve. We simply need to learn how to realize when we are lost in thought and gently, but firmly, come back to the present moment. It takes practice and patience. Now, mindfulness will not change the events of our lives, but it will transform our interpretations, experiences and relationships to those events. It won't fix us, but it will help us understand our own minds and if we can have a better understanding of our own minds, we can start to understand others, including our employees, coworkers and clients. It's the equivalent of flipping the light switch in the dark and seeing everything more clearly. If we can practice mindfulness consistently, we can transform our workplace into the place it deserves to be. A place that is heart centered, healthy and restorative. A place where we can shine brightly and illuminate everyone and everything in our path. We can all have a Firefly Culture at work.

I think the firefly has much to teach us. All we have to do is remember to be the light.

—*Camille*

Part One

"Corporate America needs THIS."

"International corporations need THIS."

"My boss would really benefit from THIS."

"My employees should have a training session on THIS."

"THIS will help me be a more effective leader."

"THIS would help with my anxiety at work."

"THIS will help me focus, relax and remain calm during the day."

"THIS will help me make better decisions."

"THIS can help me wake up and appreciate my life and remain in the present moment."

What is THIS? . . .

THIS is mindfulness in the workplace.

THE CONCEPT OF MINDFULNESS is gaining traction and recognition in the business world as a practice that can help reduce anxiety, organize thoughts, and manage stress. Many business professionals around the world have recognized the power of this practice and are creating wellness programs and hosting seminars within their workplaces related to this topic. Top executives are finding benefits, especially in their own personal leadership journey, by using this material to become better leaders and by incorporating different leadership styles and traits including those that are more empowering, compassionate, and transformational in nature. Executive coaches are now offering mentorship and coaching services to businesses that incorporate mindfulness within their curriculum.

Today, companies are developing internal resources and programs to help keep their employees minds healthy. Investing in their employees' emotional well-being provides many benefits, and it is arguably just as important as investing in their professional skills and physical health. There is less absenteeism, more engagement, and people are generally happier. This leads to increased productivity, better performance, and less employee turnover. Many businesses are interested in practicing corporate social responsibility and many already have this training in place, as part of their commitment to employee wellness and corporate social responsibility. In this way, companies give back to their employees, as well as make a social investment in them. Examples include business titans such as Google, Nike, and Apple. These companies offer mindfulness training and meditation classes to their employees as a health benefit due to its notable advantages which are documented by many large research firms.

There are many misconceptions about mindfulness and we should start by addressing these theories. Some people think that mindfulness is simply an ancient practice tied to an era, religion, culture, or group of people. Some think that the end result or goal of mindfulness training will bring about a constant state of bliss. And others think that in order to practice mindfulness you have to stop your thoughts completely. Well, let's just say, don't believe everything you hear. That's not what mindfulness is.

Let's debunk some of the myths by explaining what mindfulness is not:

- Mindfulness is not related to a new age movement, cult or organization.
- The goal is not to stop our thoughts and remain in a constant state of bliss.
- Mindfulness is not the same as meditation.
- You do not have to be a natural at it; it can be learned.
- It is not a religion and does not require you to adopt a foreign faith or give up a religious faith.

First of all, mindfulness is not obscure or exotic. We're not going to be twisting our legs into pretzels and chanting mantras for weeks on end. It is not a movement and does not belong to any cult or organization. In addition, it's certainly not about stopping your thoughts and trying to get to a place of total Zen, or 'zenning out' where nothing ever bothers you and you're in a constant state of bliss.

Another myth about mindfulness is that it is synonymous with meditation, that they are one and the same. Meditation is one way of cultivating mindfulness—it's a *means*. There are many types of meditations that do different things and focus on different aspects, just like there are different exercise machines in a gym that develop different muscles. Mindful meditations are designed to develop an attentive, open, curious and caring attitude in relation to our moment-to-moment experience. Meditation is the path, not the goal. Best of all, it is a skill that can be learned. And just like any skill, it takes practice and patience.

Most importantly, mindfulness is not a religion. Practicing it does not require giving up a religious faith or adopting a foreign faith. If you choose to make it a spiritual practice, so be it. That's your prerogative. It's certainly not required; however, in many people's opinions, the practice of mindfulness enhances the spiritual experience.

So, what exactly *is* mindfulness? It's actually pretty simple.

A great starting point would be to consult the work of one of the world's leading experts in the field, Dr. Jon Kabat-Zinn, an American Emeritus Professor of Medicine, and the creator of the "Mindfulness-Based Stress Reduction Program" (MBSR Program) at the University of Massachusetts. According to Dr. Jon Kabat-Zinn, the definition of mindfulness is, "Paying attention in a particular way: on purpose, in the present moment, and non-judgmentally."

That's it. Be here now. Simple right? But simple isn't always easy.

The purpose of practicing mindfulness is to be fully present and in the present moment—in other words, being aware of where we are and what we are doing. Not being overly reactive to what's going on around us and coming from a place of compassion, understanding, and empathy—very critical especially in relation to the workplace. And when we can start living like this—in a moment-by-moment awareness, we are able to face, head-on, the various ups and downs, the storms of our lives with ease, because we are coming from a place of deep calmness and serenity. We become fluid; we flow like water; we adapt; we change; we move; and, we are flexible—not rigid. We live in the present moment and we begin to light up from within. We become like the firefly.

We all have the capacity to be fully present. We can all cultivate these qualities with simple practices, both formal and informal, that are scientifically proven to benefit us in many ways. Growing research has shown that when we train our brains to be mindful, we become more creative, more innovative, we focus better, we become calmer and more patient. Imagine how this may benefit your workplace—the people around you, the people you interact with, your day to day tasks.

There are also several health benefits worth noting. Research has also shown that being more mindful helps lower blood pressure, reduce stress and anxiety and also helps with depression. By practicing mindfulness consistently, we literally wake up to our lives and appreciate what's happening right now. We begin to live in a state of gratitude. We begin to live in the present moment. We begin to appreciate our lives, non-judgmentally. As we practice, these shifts will naturally spill over into all aspects of our lives, including our home life, work life, our relationships with our friends, family, coworkers, employees and clients.

By practicing mindfulness, we begin to have a different relationship or experience with life. Mind you, nothing on the outside changes, it's just that our experience to different situations change. We become more grounded and less attached to the distractions and disturbances of our lives. We also become less attached to material things. We have more focus on things that are most important in our lives. We no longer cling to or obsess over negative thoughts that upset our inner balance. We turn off the vicious cycle, the never ending repetition, the endless loop that plays in our minds.

Interestingly enough, we can practice mindfulness during everyday activities such as washing the dishes, preparing a meal, gardening or even holding a team meeting. It can be done in different places, such as sitting at our desks, at home on the couch, or in the middle of a busy airport. Mindfulness helps us put some space between ourselves and our reactions to what is occurring in the present moment. It creates a pause. Applying this in the context of the workplace is very beneficial. It would allow for people to think before speaking, make better decisions, be more compassionate and considerate of others. Ultimately, it can help build better relationships, establish trust, create stronger teams, and make the workplace more positive and productive.

Incorporating Mindfulness Into Your Day

Now that we've established how transformational mindfulness can be, let's dig in and start practicing. We'll start with four simple informal steps to incorporate mindfulness into your day:

1. Stop and observe the present moment as is.

The aim is not to quiet the mind and achieve a state of calm. The aim is simply to pay attention to the present moment without judgment. Simple right? But again, simple isn't always easy. For starters, try paying attention to this moment right now by asking yourself these three questions: What can I see, what can I hear, what can I feel? Whenever you are lost in thought, try tuning in to your senses. It will bring you back to the present moment.

2. Notice your distracting thoughts.

When you start paying attention and focus your awareness on the present moment, you'll notice distracting thoughts will come in. Sometimes they seem obscure, other times they feel invasive. Acknowledge the thoughts and then, let them go. Don't follow the thought, just notice it. Label the thought or the emotion if you like: "judgment," "fear," "remembering," "planning," "worry." Then, gently let it go. Remember, it's just a thought.

3. Return to the present moment.

You'll have continuous distracting thoughts. Again and again, your attention will wander. As soon as you realize this has happened, gently acknowledge it, make a mental note of what distracted you, and bring your attention back to this moment.

4. Don't judge your thoughts.

There will be a tendency to judge yourself when you begin your practice. Be kind to yourself. Don't turn your judgments into yet something else to ruminate over. Remember, it's a new practice and just like anything else, it will take some time to get used to. Give yourself some space to learn and grow. Results will accrue over time.

That's it for the informal practice. Pay attention to the present moment. When thoughts arise, acknowledge them, label them, let them go, and bring your attention back to present moment. Non-judgmentally. You can practice anywhere, anytime. Why not start now? You can start practicing informally throughout the day without having to carve out a special time for it. Mindfulness is available to us in every moment, however formal practice is through meditation.

Practicing Mindfulness Through Meditation

One of the core practices based on the Mindfulness Based Stress Reduction program is a sitting meditation called "Awareness of Breath." This meditation can provide a way to stop all the "doing" and just "be." It will give you time to dwell in a state of relaxation and well-being and to remember who you are. It will give you the strength and self-knowledge to go back to the "doing" from a place of inner stillness, clarity and with a balanced mind. It can give you the confidence to believe in yourself, and believe in the power you have to shape your world and the world around you.

For many of us, our minds wander and jump from one thing to

another. We multitask because we work in places that are very fast-paced environments. It is looked at as a strength if you can do this, however in reality we lose focus and our thoughts become scattered. Many of us are glued to our electronic devices, constantly checking emails, messages, notifications and social media on a minute-by-minute basis. Some of us are into instant gratification, with smartphones now serving as an "all things possible" electronic device, e.g., shopping tool, messaging, phoning, photography and working device. It's no wonder we lose our focus. These habits and this lifestyle make it difficult to keep our awareness focused for any length of time unless we train ourselves to stabilize and calm our own minds.

Practicing mindfulness—the Awareness of Breath or Sitting Meditation—teaches us to observe our minds intentionally and let our experiences unfold from moment to moment and accept them as they are. It does not ask you to reject your thoughts or suppress or control them—just to focus on your breathing.

Interestingly enough, when we take time daily to practice this meditation, we realize we have little awareness of the incessant and relentless activity of our own mind and how much we are driven by it. We can take control of our mind but it needs some practice. At first, it takes some time to get comfortable with just being with your own mind. Being comfortable in this space sometimes requires us to observe and be quiet, as well as be in the right mental space. Sometimes it requires us to be in a certain part of our homes or workplaces. Yes, the external environment does make a difference for some people. But as we make time each day for a formal meditation practice, we see we are able to incorporate this anywhere. We also see the benefits:

- ⑤ We begin to calm our hearts and minds and find an inner balance to face the storms of our lives with ease.

🜍 We become aware of our fears and pain, yet at the same time become grounded and empowered by a connection to something deeper within ourselves, a wisdom that helps us discover inner peace.

🜍 We *re-tool* our minds and remind ourselves how precious the present moment is AS IS.

🜍 We remember who we are and think more positively and optimistically overall. The power of this is infinite.

If you can tap into this power, the world really is your oyster, your playground, your place for serenity, growth, and development. A place where you can constantly improve, work towards ambitious goals and be fully fulfilled both at home and at work.

Now, meditation is not a passive process. In this world and electronic age, it takes a great deal of energy to regulate your attention and remain calm and non-reactive, but it is increasingly important. Ironically, mindfulness does not involve trying to get anywhere or feel anything special. There is no end goal. It involves allowing yourself to be where you already are and to become familiar with your own experience, moment by moment.

Past and Future Tripping

*W*hen you start paying attention to where your mind is from moment to moment, you'll notice that a lot of your time and energy is spent clinging to memories, regretting the past, or planning for the future, and then, of course, worrying and fantasizing about the future. What do you want to happen, what might happen, what did happen? Will I get that promotion? Will they hire me? Did my contribution to the meeting make an impact? Do people like me? Did I say something wrong or incorrect? Did they like my work? If another offer comes, should I resign from my current job? Past and future tripping. We tend to live in a state of unconsciousness or unawareness that can cause us to miss much of what is beautiful and meaningful in our lives right here and right now.

Remember that research from Harvard? We are lost in thought 47% of the time. Can you believe that? We are walking around unconscious almost half our lives. That being said, we are on a mission to lower that percentage tremendously and actually enjoy the life that we're living right now and we truly hope you'll join us. Throughout this book we'll be guiding you through core practices based on the acclaimed Mindfulness-Based Stress Reduction program. With the introduction of this first meditation comes the knowledge that there is a way of being, of living your life that can be more joyful and abundant than it might otherwise be. This is called the way of mindfulness and our hope is that we can help you bring these beautiful concepts to all aspects of your life, and begin shining your light on everyone you meet. Our intention is to help you build your own *Firefly Culture, Illuminate Your Workplace By Tuning In to Mindfulness!*

Let's start with the Awareness of Breath or Sitting Meditation.

*f you haven't meditated before, here are some guidelines to help you:

First, find a quiet place where you can be alone or where you won't be interrupted. This could be a corner of your bedroom, the bathroom, a nook in your kitchen, your garden, or even the front seat of your car.

Next, sit comfortably. There's no need to twist your legs into an uncomfortable position. Sit in whatever position feels natural to you.

Now, close your eyes or lower them to block out any distractions.

Finally, take three deep breaths. Breathe in through your nose and breathe out through your mouth. Bring your awareness to your breath. Not trying to change anything, not trying to go anywhere. Just focusing on your breath. After centering yourself in a comfortable position with a peaceful mind, read the following meditation to yourself.

Sitting Meditation Script[1]

(Also known as Awareness of Breath Meditation[2])

This segment guides you through a sitting meditation with breath as the primary object of awareness.

Arranging to spend this time in a comfortable but attentive posture, preferably sitting up without letting back for support, if that's possible for you. Sitting in a dignified posture, head balanced on shoulders, arms and hands resting in a comfortable position.

This is a time to switch from our normal mode of doing and moving and reacting to one of *simply being*. Just be attentive to what's happening within your own awareness, right here and right now.

As you sit, *just noticing sensations of breath.*

Just noticing how your abdomen moves on each in-breath and out-breath, the movement of air through your nostrils, a slight movement of chest and shoulders.

Just bring your awareness to your breath cycle and wherever it is the most vivid, whether it be your tummy, your chest or your shoulders, or the movement of air through your nostrils.

Noticing the entirety of breath, from the movement of the air coming in, and filling the lungs, and extending the abdomen slightly, the movement of air going out, and being aware of the pause, the stopping point, in between the in-breath and the out-breath, and the out-breath and the next in-breath. It's all one movement, even through the changing of direction; just notice where that pause is and seeing to what degree you can be aware of your whole entire cycle. Recognizing that each part of the cycle is different from the other part and this time through maybe different from the last time through, and each one is absolutely unique in its own way, if you pay attention.

You'll notice your attention from time to time shifting away from breath. The mind may wander into fantasies, or memories, thoughts of the day, worries that you might have, things you need to do. *Without giving yourself a hard time* when you notice that that happened, gently but firmly bring your attention back to the sensations of breathing. The actual physical sensations of breath as it moves through your body.

Being aware of where the mind goes, gently shifting your awareness to sensations of breath.

Notice the tendency to want to control your breathing. Let the quality of attention be *light and easy*, one of *simply observing and noticing,* just as if you were on a float on a *gently undulating* sea, where you're up with one wave and down with the next. You don't control the duration of the wave, or the depth between the waves; you're just riding.

And just *gently coming back* to sensations of breathing.

You may notice that there are sounds of traffic or movement, or something else going on. *Just notice* that your attention has moved to that perception of sound. Just staying with it long enough to notice the quality of the sound. Sound is vibration, tone, volume or intensity. Being aware of the mind to label sound, as traffic, or as voices, or as music and coming closer to the sound as it hits your ear drums. The quality or pitch or rhythm or intensity. *Separating out the actual reception of sound from the labels* we put on it.

And if you've been paying attention to sound or noticing that you've gotten off to noticing the perception of sound, bring your attention once again back to breath, letting your breath be your anchor of awareness, so that each time your awareness goes somewhere else, just gently coming back to the breath, without judgment or any upset if you can do that. If you see that your attention has gone somewhere else, just coming back to the breath.

And noticing the tendency to have an opinion about things. About liking the way things are going right now, not liking it, finding it uncomfortable; that too can be an object of awareness. Just noticing that you have an opinion about things often. So, that's my liking mind; it's liking this. So that's my critical mind that would rather have things be different than they are. That too can be noticed. Building the capacity to notice liking or disliking and *not to have to do anything about it. How freeing that is!*

And as you notice that happening, just bring your awareness to the physical sensations of breath, wherever it's most vivid for you, *just riding the entire cycle, one cycle after another.*

You may notice your attention shifting to body sensations, of achiness or discomfort or tension.

As you notice these sensations of discomfort that happen for you, there's several things which can be done with just the sensation, and one is to, if it's one that can be remedied by shifting a little bit, one way to deal with the sensation is to allow yourself to shift, but in doing that, first becoming aware of the sensation, noticing precisely where the tension or the achiness might be, and once you're aware of where that is, developing an intention to move, and moving mindfully, and with full intent to make that motion. That's one way to deal with strong sensation.

A second way, and neither one is better than the other is, as long as full awareness is brought to all parts, is to notice that sensation, noticing it in its fullness, being curious about the extent of it, how your experience of it is at the moment, the actual physical sensations of tension or of throbbing, or of tightness, or of pulling, or tingling. And the second way of dealing with it is just to notice that it's possible to stay for a moment longer with that sensation, *experienced as pure sensation, without the labels* of discomfort, or of tension, or of achiness; just noticing just where it is. Noticing your experience of it and *staying with it, without having to react to it,* just for the moment.

And if your attention keeps getting called back to that area of intense sensation, knowing you have those two choices; of forming an intention to do something about it, and mindfully doing it, but forming intention first; or bringing your attention and intention right in to it.

Be curious about it:

How big is it? How long is it? What quality does it have? How is it changing over time?

And wherever the mind goes, in terms of thoughts, to liking or disliking, perceptions or sensation, or hearing of sound, or feelings of peace or of sadness, or frustration, or of anticipation; just noticing these raw thought forms, and bringing awareness to sensations to the movement of breath.

And being curious about breath, observing that no two breaths are exactly the same.

And seeing if it is possible to have a friendly attitude toward whatever comes into your awareness. Now if your mind has gone off on a fantasy or a thought, or a judgment, or a worry, or a sensation, or a sound, just in a *friendly way* notice that this is happening and coming back to the breath. Recognizing that the *entire cycle of awareness is important* to this experience, including the movement from breath, and including the coming back.

And *nothing to do but ride the waves* of breath.

Seeing if it is possible in those moments when your awareness is gone somewhere else, noticing how that flicker of attention happens, that moment when you realize it is somewhere else, somewhere other than breath, and at that moment seeing if it is possible of having an *attitude of celebration, of congratulation*, of recognition that *this is a moment of awareness.* You acknowledge yourself for noticing you've gone somewhere else. And just easily bring your attention back to breath in a *friendly* and *non-judgmental* way.

As this meditation comes to an end, recognizing that you spent this time intentionally aware of your moment-to-moment experience, nourishing and strengthening your ability to be with *whatever comes your way.* Building the capacity for opening the senses to the vividness, to the aliveness of the present moment. Expanding your skill to be *curious, and available, about whatever presents itself, without judgment.*

Notes

Notes

Notes

Part Two

*A*t the end of the day, ask yourself these three questions:

- ♪ Did I love enough?
- ♪ Did I laugh enough?
- ♪ Did I make a difference?

If you can answer "yes" to all three questions as it pertains to your work life, you can rest assured you have had a successful day, with success being defined as living a life you are proud of.

Many of us think work should be drudgery. Work is just something we do to bring home a paycheck. We work to live and we live to work. It's all cyclical and it is like being on a hamster wheel. Every day is the same old grind. Make money to pay the bills—another day, another dollar. Work is something we are trained we 'have to do' rather than we 'want to do.'

Truthfully, work can be so much more. We can make a difference in people's lives and create some positive impact. We constantly hear about people who say 'I've never worked a day in my life because I love what I do.' Can you believe some people actually feel this way and live their life with that mindset? This too can be you. But how?

The truth is work can be both a fulfilling and positive experience. Work can be filled with love and laughter. Work can be filled with joyfulness and jubilation. Work can be something we look forward to, rather than dread, on Monday mornings. It can be something we can greet with positive emotions and also be thankful for. Work can be a place where we make a difference and create a positive change in people's lives. For this to take place, we have to get anchored in the present moment. We have to find a way to reduce stress and anxiety so we can make better decisions—decisions that come from a clear and balanced mind. We all want to have the ability to do this. To do this, we have to find a way to become more thoughtful leaders and lead with excellence and compassion. We have to find a way to incorporate attitudes such as forgiveness, tolerance, patience and gratitude into our daily work lives so we can better serve our co-workers, our employees, our clients. We can accomplish this through mindfulness. If we can practice these beautiful concepts, we CAN make a difference and change the world. Right from our desks at work.

Being mindful helps us train our attention to be in the present moment. When we practice mindfulness, we are exercising that part of our attention "muscle" and becoming mentally fit. We can take more control over our focus of attention and choose what we want to focus on, rather than allowing our attention to be dominated by that which distresses us and takes us away from the present moment. Worry, stress and anxiety: they all can be overcome through mindfulness.

In Part One, formal and informal mindful training was outlined, with mindful meditations being formal. We learned the Awareness of

Breath Meditation, which is simply paying attention to our breath and allowing thoughts and feelings to come and go without getting caught up in them. Releasing these thoughts is key. Don't hang on to them or obsess over them. When we consistently practice the awareness of breath meditation, we begin to realize that our thoughts have a pull to them, especially negative or distressful thoughts. They tend to occur and reoccur from time to time. During mindful meditations, the goal is to simply acknowledge that we are having a thought, but we are not our thoughts. We are the awareness behind the thought. Like a movie, we're watching our thoughts. We are the watcher. Consistently having a meditation practice will train us to see this. This practice will create calmness and acceptance and allow us to have a different perspective of our life and the stress that we all have. Now, stress is a part of life and much of it comes from the workplace and from what we consider high-pressure jobs (which are in any and every field). We can't get away from it, but we can have a different relationship to stress. The stress doesn't go away; we just experience it differently.

Workplace Relationships

Consider your relationship with your boss. You may have to report to them daily, but how you approach those matters and how you handle issues is what changes. The thought process and perspective also changes. For instance, leading with compassion will bring out the best in you and others. Being more patient will allow you to grasp more understanding and deal with difficult situations and difficult people.

Most people that are difficult to work with are not upset at you or any one thing. It is a combination of things, and they most likely lead lives that are chaotic and disorganized. Disorganization may be taken in the literal sense, like a mess in the office. But, it can also be thought of within the mind. Scattered thinking, being neither here nor there, worrying about the past and future. Most stress and disorganization of thoughts are caused by not living in the present moment, not having focus, and always being fretful over the past or the future.

Think about it. What are you upset about right now? What is your current stress button? We all have it. But ask yourself this…Is it happening right now? Why am I so anxious or upset about this situation that isn't even occurring right now? For instance, worrying about a promotion and feeling bad about not getting it before the decision is made. Maybe it's concern over performance evaluations before the results are in. Or perhaps the issue is wondering if you will be fired when there is no reason to think so. Stop for a moment to examine your thoughts. Don't judge the thought or allow negative thoughts to enter. Just sit back and watch the movie that is playing in your mind. Are you right here, right now? Or are you in the past, ruminating about a situation that occurred, or in the future worrying about what might happen? It's been said a positive mindset brings positive outcomes. In other words, if you put positivity out in the world, you will draw positive energy to you and exceptional leaders have mastered this. We all know who we would love to work for or which teacher we liked the most when we were growing up. People are drawn to those who have mastered this concept, creating a positive energy force field.

By having a consistent mindful practice, we begin to see that we can train ourselves to live fully in the present moment. There are different ways to approach mindfulness and the attitude that we bring to our practice will be crucial. It's the seeds for planting a firm foundation in which we can begin to cultivate a strong sense of who we are. We begin to know ourselves better and become more accepting of ourselves, which in turn helps us to become more accepting of others. When we accept ourselves and others, we begin to see ourselves as we truly are, not as we would like to be. It is then, that we can begin to live our lives more joyfully and awaken to our true purpose. It is then that we can illuminate our workplace and cultivate a Firefly Culture.

The Seven Attitudes of Mindfulness

*A*ccording to Jon Kabat-Zinn in his best-selling book *Full Catastrophe Living*,[1] there are seven main attitudes that we should bring to our mindfulness practice. They should be cultivated consciously when we practice, as they will be the soil in which we effectively bring awareness to our goal of illuminating our workplace. When we can incorporate these attitudes into our daily routine, they will help our mindfulness practice grow and flourish.

1. Non-Judging

Let's begin with a definition of non-judging as it relates to our mindfulness practice. Non-judging is the ability to step back and be the witness to our own experience. In essence, it's resisting the urge to label the experience. To do this requires us to become aware of the constant stream of thoughts and judgments that cloud our minds and consume our days. Both inner and outer experiences are judged day-in and day-out by us, without even realizing it. An example of inner experiences would be judging co-workers, people around you, or the leaders in your organization. Outer experiences can be seen as disagreements with co-workers, confrontations, and hostile work situations in the workplace. These are situations that are worth stepping back from, but how might we do this? When we start to pay attention to the constant stream of activity of our own mind, we are shocked to discover we are constantly judging our experiences.

All experiences are labeled in our minds. We react to people, events, and situations and label them "good" or "bad," "liking" or "disliking". We do this all the time at networking events, in meetings, during presentations—we judge and sometimes we find ourselves going way off track. How do we come back? How do we find a more effective way of handling our judgments in our lives? The first thing we need to do is to become aware of these judgments, without being too harsh on ourselves. Don't judge your judgments! Pull yourself back and just observe. Watch your thoughts and become the gentle witness to your experience without the need to label each one. It's the first step towards liberation from the seemingly strong pull these thoughts have on us. Another judgment you might have is of your meditation practice, especially when you begin your mindful meditations. You might start having thoughts like, "Am I doing this right? What am I supposed to feel? I don't think this is doing anything. This is boring." That's a judgment. Recognize that you are having a judgmental thought, and during the meditation come back to your breath. No-judgment.

2. Patience

We are always in situations at work that require us to be patient. Sometimes it's a meeting starting late, or ending late. Sometimes it's deadlines not being met or performance goals not being achieved. Other times it's dealing with co-workers or clients and their issues. In any case, patience is required. Sometimes daily. Sometimes hourly. Sometimes moment by moment. When we practice the attitude of patience, it helps us realize and accept the fact that life unfolds naturally. Why rush to get the promotion you are not ready for, as maybe it's not the appointed time. Why try to overexert yourself, chasing after something when there is time. Why jump immediately to a solution when coworkers or clients truly need space to come to terms with their issues? Let life unfold organically. Each moment is your life in that moment. Patience can be a very good quality to invoke when our mind is agitated. Whether its anger or impatience toward your boss, frustrations with your co-workers, it can help us accept that our minds wander, while also reminding us we don't have to get caught up in its travels. Patience is known as a form of wisdom, and as we continue to bring this attitude to our mindfulness practice and to our workplace, we remember that just like a butterfly, things unfold in their own time.

3. Beginner's Mind

Beginner's Mind is a concept taken from Zen Buddhism. The phrase is discussed in the book *Zen Mind, Beginner's Mind* by Shunryu Suzuki.[2] Suzuki was a spiritual teacher and founding father of Zen in America.

What exactly is Beginner's Mind? It's the concept of dropping our expectations and perceived ideas about something, and seeing things with an open mind and fresh clear eyes . . . just like a beginner. In the book Suzuki writes, "In the beginner's mind there are many possibilities, in the expert's mind there are few." To practice this concept, we need to start seeing what is actually happening, and we need to come at it from a blank slate. When we cultivate this practice of Beginner's Mind, we begin to see everything as if for the first time. We see things with fresh eyes, like when you start a new job—you meet new people; it's a new environment; you gain new experiences. This mindset allows us to be receptive to new possibilities and break free of our expectations based on our past experiences. It reminds us that each moment is unique and contains unique possibilities.

Too often we let our thinking and beliefs about a person or a problem prohibit us from seeing things as they really are. To practice this attitude, next time you are with someone who is familiar, ask yourself this: Am I seeing this person with fresh eyes, or am I only seeing a reflection of my own thoughts about this person? What preconceived notions do I hold? Try this with problems when they arise. For instance, if the company you work for is not making its sales target, alter your thinking and consider this: Are you seeing the problem with a clear and uncluttered mind or are you seeing it through the veil of your own thoughts and opinions? Are you rehashing old patterns of behaviors and coming at it from the same mindset? If you are open to a new way of thinking, then how can you fix it? Starting with the Beginner's Mind is important. Then and only then can you design solutions to a problem, from a mind that is uncluttered, relaxed and receptive.

4. Trust

The foundation of any relationship begins with trust, including the relationship you have with yourself. Trusting yourself will build confidence, which in turn will allow you to make better decisions and ultimately reduce stress. It's better to trust in your own intuition and your own thoughts and ideas, even if you encounter some hiccups along the way.

Have you heard the phrase 'trust your gut'? In essence, your gut instinct can help guide you if you are in tune with yourself. If something doesn't feel right to you, honor your own feelings. Follow those feelings.

Sometimes we discount our own feelings because some authority or group of people think or say something different. At work, sometimes we feel inclined to follow what the boss says and not share our own thoughts or ideas because of the power difference. The attitude of trusting yourself and your own wisdom is very important to your meditation practice.

Some people get caught up in what others think and actually believe these people must be wiser and more advanced. In the workplace, it could be due to age, education level, gender—aspects that we link to intelligence levels. This attitude is completely contrary to the spirit of meditation, which emphasizes being your own person.

The reason for practicing mindfulness through meditation is to become more fully yourself. It's important to be open and receptive to others, however, at the end of the day, you still have to live your own life. As we practice the attitude of trusting in ourselves at work, daily, we naturally begin to trust others.

5. Non-Striving

Let's face it. Everything we do at work has a goal or purpose. Every day, every minute, we need to get something accomplished or make something happen. Push, push, push—make it work! This can be an obstacle in meditation, because meditation is different from any other activity in life, especially in the workplace.

Although it takes a lot of work and energy, ultimately meditation is about non-doing. This concept of non-doing or non-striving is the total opposite of what we consider to be a successful strategy at work. Meditation has no goal other than for you to be yourself. Here's the catch: You already are! For example, if you sit down to meditate and you think, "Okay, after ten minutes of meditation, I'm going to be more relaxed; I'm going to be stress free; I'm going to handle obstacles at work with ease," then you're introducing the fact that you're not okay right now, and you have to get to the place of being okay. This actually undermines the whole concept of mindfulness, which is simply paying attention to whatever is happening in the present moment.

If you're tense and stressed, then just pay attention to your body and where you feel the tension. If you feel pain in your shoulders, in your back, in your forehead, pay attention to the pain as best you can. If you sense the feeling of criticizing or judging yourself, then observe your judging mind. Just watch. The best way to achieve any goals at work, such as being less stressed, is to back off from the striving for results and instead focus on seeing things as they are, in this moment. With patience and a regular meditation practice, movement towards reaching your goals will happen with ease. This movement unfolds organically within you and will ultimately soften any tension that has built up inside of you.

Using an approach of non-striving at work can have many beneficial effects. There is no need to push or try so hard. Let things evolve naturally. Hard work and effort is always needed, but overexertion is not required to reach every goal. Balance is the key.

6. Acceptance

Acceptance is seeing things as they really are in the present moment. An example at work would be if you have to call in sick one day, accept that you're taking a sick day. Life will go on. Most of the time, before acceptance, we have to go through denial and anger. We waste a lot of time and energy denying and resisting what already is. "I can't call in sick. The boss will kill me! That report won't get done. People are counting on me for that presentation." Denial and anger at its best. When we do this, we are basically trying to change things or force situations into what we want them to be, which only results in more tension. If you currently are in a situation that you don't like, the first thing you should do is accept it.

For example, if you accepted a job and your boss is difficult to work with, accept it and don't blame yourself for taking the job—you likely accepted it with the information you had at the time. Think of an exit strategy which is more productive. You have to accept it before you can change it. Now, acceptance does not mean you have to like everything that occurs or you have to take a passive attitude towards things and relinquish your principles and values. It doesn't mean you have to be satisfied with things as they are or tolerate things that irritate you. Acceptance is a willingness to see things as they are right now.

You are much more likely to know what to do to change things when you have a clear picture of what is actually happening, rather than when your vision is clouded by your minds judgments, biases and prejudices. When in doubt, remember the serenity prayer: "Grant me the serenity to accept the things I cannot change, the courage to change the things I can, and the wisdom to know the difference." It's worth repeating and worth posting on your whiteboard at work.

7. Letting go

Letting go, or non-attachment, is fundamental to the practice of mindfulness and probably one of the hardest to cultivate. Letting go is a way of letting things be, of accepting them as they are. Whether you resigned from a job, made a mistake on a presentation, did terribly on a job interview or failed to meet a sales goal, at some point we have to let it be and let go of the negative emotions that surround the situation. We have to let things go and just allow our experience to be whatever it is: whatever is happening in the moment. Without judgment.

As we continue with our mindfulness practice, we will discover there are certain thoughts, feelings or situations that our minds seem to want to hold onto. Certain thoughts are pleasant and we try to prolong them. However, certain thoughts are not so pleasant and have a hold on us, or more of a grip on us. We attach to these thoughts and replay them over and over, like a movie. Sometimes we even create problems in our minds and then create solutions! This is a sincere waste of time—paying attention to hypothetical situations and then creating hypothetical resolutions to problems that don't even exist. For example, having a hundred back-up plans. We literally cling to these thoughts out of fear, worry and anxiety. We can feel the pull of them and sometimes they seem to be very powerful. We can get caught up in our minds and before you know it, minutes, hours, days go by. Truthfully, if we find it difficult to let go of something because it has such a strong hold on our minds, we can direct our attention to what "holding" feels like. Holding on is the opposite of letting go.

When we are willing to look at the ways we hold on or cling, it shows us a lot about its opposite. Believe it or not, letting go is not such a foreign concept. Think about it. We do it every night before we go to sleep. Now, there are times when our minds are in a frenzy and we can't seem to shut down before bed. This is a sign of extreme stress. During these times, we are unable to break free from certain thoughts because it seems like our involvement in them is so powerful. When this happens, we can practice the concept of letting go by turning to our formal meditation practice, tune into our breath and hopefully get a good night's sleep.

*W*e reached out to a few of our peers, mentors and clients about how they incorporate the seven attitudes of mindfulness into their workday. Here's a sampling of their thoughts:

"Where to begin! I recently moved to a new state and new city and was given the opportunity to manage a larger scope of the business. I knew it was going to be a challenge to my leadership skills because I had a new team and new peers that didn't know my past or what I was bringing to the table to help them excel in their current or future roles. So when I think about the seven attitudes of mindfulness, I had to practice all of them on a daily basis. When being introduced to a new team, I always look at overall results and get feedback from past leaders, but what I have learned through this journey is you need to be very mindful of not judging what others say and or feel. In the past, I knew all the players, coaches, and good or bad behaviors, and I was able to make quick sound judgments. In this situation, it was all new and I had to reflect on what I needed to accomplish.

"First and foremost, I had to understand the area and demographics, but most importantly, the team and partners I was now leading. They didn't know me, so that placed a whole other piece to the puzzle. All I had coming into this new role were current and past production reports or how a person was described to me. I have to admit, I formed some judgments before meeting them but took time to reflect on how I was going to approach each person and their team and how I wanted to make sure I had a positive outcome with no judgment. I wanted to take the time to get to know them and help them.

"After reflecting, I put a process in place to help me with getting to know my new team because I wanted to form my own opinion without judgment. This process did not take long. I met with each person, asking key questions, such as: what do they want to accomplish, what has helped them in the past, what has gotten in the way, what type of coaching has worked well and what hasn't (along with why), what are their strengths and opportunities (I never say weakness), and how I can help them. Then I flipped the tables and shared my information and my journey, opening up to their questions.

"What I uncovered was that I had people on my team who did not have the persona or skills that were presented to me. It has been a true learning experience for me because as a leader when I presented this information, I was judged for having a different opinion than what was the "norm". This is when I incorporated patience into my mindfulness because I was the new person on the team and a part of a larger leadership group, so when I formed my non-judgmental opinions about my new team, my direct manager and some partners didn't agree. So through a three to six-month period, I was patient with my team, coached and developed, but through the initial meeting with them continued to go back to the key areas we focused on—their journey, what they wanted to accomplish, and how have their strengths and opportunities improved.

"This mindfulness practice helped me increase my patience with my team and my direct leaders, but more importantly, built a stronger overall team built on trust. If the team knows you are there to support and help, no matter where they are at in their career or what they do or do not know, being non-judgmental and patient will increase the strength, trust and overall higher outcomes."

—*Mary P., Market Director, Houston, TX*

"So important to be in the moment, especially when one encounters (let's say) difficult people. Sometimes I remind myself, *'hurt people, hurt people'*. This helps me stay centered and not get dragged down by negativity. Not to mention recognizing my own hurt and not projecting it onto others"—*Kevin A., Project Manager, Tavares, FL*

"This is how I mentally prepare even for a few moments before I must take on a challenging client, employee issue, or something I know I must face:

- Take a few deep and slow breaths with eyes closed. This helps to regulate your heart rate and focus
- Clear your mind as best you can so you are least stressed.
- Having patience with others is directly tied in with our ability to control our own emotions in an out of control situation. So . . . sometimes it's best to "hit the pause button". That allows for time to pass before losing patience (and control). At work, you can do this by immediately addressing a situation if you must, but then taking time to come up with a final answer or solution.
- Listening takes patience and one must also have the patience to listen.
- Make it a point to relax your facial expression and SMILE. A relaxed smile suggests composure and patience and you should smile before heading in to address whatever you must."

—*Margaret C., Benefits Counselor, Melbourne, FL*

"The job that I am currently in has been the most challenging one to date. Mindfulness is the only thing that has helped me survive for the past year and allowed me to go into work without quitting. The area in which I really had to be fully aware of what I am doing in the present was the training. Since it is a small family-owned business in which we wear many hats, the training program was extremely accelerated. I was forced to learn things that were outside the job description for a Business Analyst. To say that the speed at which we were moving was intense was an overstatement.

"I was utterly and completely overwhelmed with the fact that the training was only conducted lecture style with no repetition or reinforcement to retain the material. Even though I provided feedback on the training, nothing was done to alter the presentation, so I knew I had to take matters into my own hands.

"In order to be completely present, I removed all objects that may cause a distraction, such as my cell phone, email, and even food. I started by counting my breaths—breathed in for a count of six breaths and out for six. I had to really focus on this. I also practiced effective listening skills in which I gave eye contact to the instructor and read their mouth as the speed of talking was well above average. I tried my best to jot down the most important lessons learned as I know it was not possible to retain all of the information. Caution was used not to write down every single statement as then I was not truly being present in the moment.

"At night, I reviewed my notes, read the technical user guide, and practiced on the software. I came to the realization that class was not enough and in order to retain and apply the information, I had to practice on my own time. I would arrive to class early and review my notes/test results from the previous day and, most importantly, have quiet time before it began to relax myself as much as possible.

"So, in summary, breath work, arriving early, quiet time before class, effective listening, and application of the material on my own helped me survive this invaluable life lesson of practicing mindfulness at the workplace." —*Jennifer M., Business Analyst, Orlando, FL*

"Since reading Camille's first book *Hippiebanker: Bringing Peace, Love and Spirituality to the Workplace*, I often hear her inspiration in my head.

"I work for a major banking firm and I am customer-facing day after day. Being a type A personality, I often find myself impatient and distracted while listening to a long-winded client. However, I am working on being more mindful of other people and being a better version of myself, so I am aware of when I am doing this. Often I find myself immediately ready to answer a question before it is being asked, which appears rude and unconcerned, therefore failing in my customer service role.

"Since listening to Camille's meditations and reading her blogs, I find myself less judgmental and more eager to listen before I respond. In fact, last week I had an elderly lady that sat at my desk for nearly an hour chatting and visiting long after her transaction was complete. I sat with her, listening and engaged. When she stood to leave, I reached out to shake her hand and she reached in and hugged me with tears in her eyes. It was evident she needed to be heard and I was there for her. At that moment I knew I was on my way to being who I want to be: a person who leads with mindfulness. I am not sure who was more grateful, my client or me."

—*Francine L., Home Lending Advisor, Rockledge, FL*

nother very useful meditation we can bring to our practice to create a Firefly Culture at work is called the Body Scan Meditation. [3]

The Body Scan Meditation is one of the core practices of the MBSR clinic. This meditation involves concentrating and moving our minds through different parts of our bodies. We start with the toes and move up through our bodies, feeling the sensations as we go and directing our breath to and from the different regions. By the time we're finished, it can feel like our entire body has dropped away and there is nothing but breath flowing all across us. As we complete the body scan, we let ourselves dwell in silence and stillness, in an awareness that may be beyond the body altogether. Then, when we are ready, we come back to our body, to a sense of it as a whole. We feel it solid again.

The idea in scanning the body is to actually feel each region and focus our mind on it and in it. We breathe in to and out from each region a few times and then let go of it in our mind's eye as our attention moves to the next region. As we let go of the sensations and any thoughts we may have had associated with it, the muscles in that region let go and release any tension we might have.

It helps to imagine that the tension is flowing out from your body on the out breath and on the in breath, you are breathing in energy, vitality and relaxation.

Through repeated practice of the body scan, we grasp the reality of our body as a whole in the present moment. This feeling of wholeness can be experienced no matter what is wrong with your body. You may have pain in some parts of your body, however, you can still have the experience of wholeness. Each time you practice, you are letting what will flow out, flow out. You don't try and force anything. If you practice being present in each moment and at the same time allowing your breathing and your attention to purify your body with awareness and a willingness to accept whatever happens, then you are truly practicing mindfulness and tapping into its power to heal.

Body Scan Meditation

*B*egin by making yourself comfortable. Sit in a chair and allow your back to be straight, but not stiff, with your feet on the ground. You could also do this practice standing or if you prefer, you can lie down and have your head supported. Your hands could be resting gently in your lap or at your side. Allow your eyes to close, or to remain open with a soft gaze.

Take several long, slow, deep breaths. Breathing in fully and exhaling slowly. Breathe in through your nose and out through your nose or mouth. Feel your stomach expand on an inhale and relax and let go as you exhale. Begin to let go of noises around you. Begin to shift your attention from outside to inside yourself. If you are distracted by sounds in the room, simply notice this and bring your focus back to your breathing.

Now slowly bring your attention down to your feet. Begin observing sensations in your feet. You might want to wiggle your toes a little, feeling your toes against your socks or shoes. Just notice, without judgment. You might imagine sending your breath down to your feet, as if the breath is traveling through the nose to the lungs and through the abdomen all the way down to your feet. And then back up again out through your nose and lungs. Perhaps you don't feel anything at all. That is fine, too. Just allow yourself to feel the sensation of not feeling anything. When you are ready, allow your feet to dissolve in your mind's eye and move your attention up to your ankles, calves, knees and thighs. Observe the sensations you are experiencing throughout your legs. Breathe into and breathe out of the legs. If your mind begins to wander during this exercise, gently notice this without judgment and bring your mind back to noticing the sensations in your legs. If you notice any discomfort, pain or stiffness, don't judge this. Just simply notice it.

Observe how all sensations rise and fall, shift and change moment to moment. Notice how no sensation is permanent. Just observe and allow the sensations to be in the moment, just as they are. Breathe into and out from the legs. Then on the next out breath, allow the legs to dissolve in your mind. And move to the sensations in your lower back and pelvis. Softening and releasing as you breathe in and out. Slowly move your attention up to your mid back and upper back. Become curious about the sensations here. You may become aware of sensations in the muscle, temperature or points of contact with furniture or the bed. With each out breath, you may let go of tension you are carrying. And then very gently shift your focus to your stomach and all the internal organs here. Perhaps you notice the feeling of clothing, the process of digestion or the belly rising or falling with each breath. If you notice opinions arising about these areas, gently let these go and return to noticing sensations.

As you continue to breathe, bring your awareness to the chest and heart region and just notice your heartbeat. Observe how the chest rises during the inhale and how the chest falls during the exhale. Let go of any judgments that may arise. On the next out breath, shift the focus to your hands and fingertips. See if you can channel your breathing into and out of this area as if you are breathing into and out from your hands. If your mind wanders, gently bring it back to the sensations in your hands.

And then, on the next out breath, shift the focus and bring your awareness up into your arms. Observe the sensations or lack of sensations that may be occurring there. You might notice some difference between the left arm and the right arm—no need to judge this. As you exhale, you may experience the arm soften and release tension. Continue to breathe and shift focus to the neck, shoulder and throat region. This is an area where we often have tension. Be with the sensations here. It could be tightness, rigidity or holding. You may notice the shoulders moving along with the breath. Let go of any thoughts or stories you are telling about this area. As you breathe, you may feel tension rolling off your shoulders. On the next out breath, shift your focus and direct your attention to the scalp, head and face. Observe all of the sensations occurring there. Notice the movement of the air as you breathe into or out of the nostrils or mouth. As you exhale, you might notice the softening of any tension you may be holding.

And now, let your attention to expand out to include the entire body as a whole. Bring into your awareness the top of your head down to the bottom of your toes. Feel the gentle rhythm of the breath as it moves through the body. As you come to the end of this practice, take a full, deep breath, taking in all the energy of this practice. Exhale fully. And when you are ready, open your eyes and return your attention to the present moment. As you become fully alert and awake, consider setting the intention that this practice of building awareness will benefit everyone you come in contact with today.

Notes

Notes

41

Notes

Part Three

Listen to the wind, it talks.
Listen to the silence, it speaks.
Listen to your heart, it knows.

—Native American Proverb

To RECAP, in Parts One and Two we covered the benefits of mindfulness and the seven attitudes to bring to our mindfulness practice. It is hoped you have found this to be useful in your journey toward learning and practicing mindfulness. In Part Three we will focus more on the benefits of mindfulness in the workplace, work stress, and practical tips and simple tools to transform your work environment into the place it deserves to be.

Let's start with the proven benefits of mindfulness in the workplace:

- ♪ Dealing with challenges more effectively.

- ♪ Ability to think more clearly.

- ♪ Ability to focus more closely on the task at hand.

- ♪ Improved concentration.

- ♪ Increased productivity.

- ❦ Improved interpersonal skills.

- ❦ Improved communication skills.

- ❦ Emotions are managed or 'in-check'.

- ❦ Recognition and realization of internal and external distractions.

At work, we are constantly inundated with various challenges: deadlines, priorities, meeting goals, maintaining our relationships with our colleagues, conference calls to attend, and the list goes on. Mindfulness allows us to think more clearly, logically, and provides the patience required to deal with all kinds of challenges before us. If mastered correctly, it gives us a few minutes of lead time or 'think time' before handling situations and allows us to think of better solutions to the challenges we face.

Mindfulness will also strengthen your state of mind and help you develop focus. Improvements in these areas are beneficial to all workplaces. It will improve decision making and communication skills so you can work with clarity of purpose and a balanced mind. This is the power of mindfulness.

Addressing Work-Related Stress

*W*hat is the number one cause of stress? If you really get down to it, it's worry and anxiety about situations that are not even happening in the present moment. Most of us spend our days not paying attention to our lives as they are unfolding. We are living in the past or future. We are lost in thought (47% of the time!) With mindfulness, you'll shift from a habit of continually projecting into the future or ruminating about the past.

Training your attention to stay with the experience that is actually occurring helps the mind's ability to stay focused and aware. We begin to see what is truly present, not what we wish or fear is present.

A person can experience job stress at any level and at any pay grade in a major company or in any small business. The level of stress you experience depends on your perspective and how your mind interprets things. In other words, it's your attitude that matters and whether you are able to flow with changes. It's best to be like water—go with the flow. You need to be like one of those flexible trees: when a windstorm comes, they sway with the wind. They are truly flexible. The trees that are firm are not like this; they generally break apart when a windstorm comes along.

Even if you have a job with a good salary and feel safe or secure in your position, you are never completely in control as the law of impermanence will always apply. Nothing is forever and the only thing constant is change. The trick is to remain centered and balanced inside, no matter what happens outside. That's where a mindfulness practice comes in. It helps alleviate stress by constantly bringing you back to the present moment; in this way, it is a constant reminder. But the mind needs practice and the mind needs training. Think of this practice as maintenance of the mind. As we develop this practice, we are able to handle stress by dealing with each situation as it is presented to us in that moment with clarity and a balanced mind.

Work stress in itself can be greatly reduced by a commitment to cultivating calmness and awareness at your job. Also, it can be reduced by letting mindfulness guide your actions on a daily basis. Bringing your meditation and mindfulness practice to your work life can make for major improvements in the quality of your life at work as well as your interpersonal relationships with people. And by the way, you don't have to get out of a stressful job for your work life to change. You can change your environment yourself. By working on your inner life and keeping a positive mindset, you will see the benefits outside of you.

This is not to say that staying in a highly stressful or toxic workplace is okay as long as you practice mindfulness. No, toxic workplaces are a deal-breaker. It simply means, if you are unable to change the stressful conditions in your workplace, mindfulness can be used as a tool to change your relationship with stress and it starts with practice.

Remember, work can become a vehicle that you are using to learn and grow. Obstacles become opportunities, frustrations become opportunities to practice patience; power struggles become lessons in unawareness in other people and yourself. When you use the Seven Attitudes of Mindfulness that we learned about in Part Two and bring them into your workplace, you begin to change your relationship to stress. You change your experience.

Now, mind you, stress is always going to be a common thread in any workplace. There will always be deadlines, sales goals to meet, people to manage, unreasonable timelines to adhere to, reports to get done, work to be presented, bosses to please, and more. However, we can change our attitude and outlook. When we do this, it's a game changer. As Wayne Dyer once said, "When you change the way you look at things, the things you look at change."

Five Actions to Reduce Stress in the Workplace

*H*ow do we begin the process of turning our workplace into a Firefly Culture? Let's start with five suggestions for reducing work stress:

1. **Start each day with a short mindful meditation.**

If you can, meditate in the morning before heading off to work for 10–15 minutes. Then, when you get to work, sit for a moment quietly at your desk for a few moments and contemplate your day. Ask yourself "How am I facing my workday today?" Set an intention for the day. Think of how you want your day to unfold. For example, you can set the intention that "Today will flow with ease; I'll accomplish everything that needs to get done today." Next, tune in to the moment with a short breathing exercise. Just bringing your awareness to your breath for one minute will set you up for success.

2. Make your "To Do" list.

Go over your list and remind yourself that it may or may not happen that way. Things change and that's okay. The attitude that you bring to work is much more important to each task.

What's more important than your "To Do" list is your "To Be" list. Your "To Be" list is exactly that—what am I "being" as I am doing my job. Contemplate that one. Am I being patient? Am I being compassionate? Am I being a good listener? Am I being judgmental? It's a moment to moment awareness. Your "To Be" list is SO much more important than your "To Do" list.

When challenges occur, ask yourself: Am I more concerned with being right and winning the argument, or is it my priority to find a solution? When you come from a place of acting from your heart, your defenses will come down as well as your stress levels.

3. Remember, you can begin to bring your mindfulness practice to work in small bite size pieces.

You might even want to start a practice of mindful eating. Maybe take your lunch outside in nature. So many of us rush through our lunch just to put out the next fire that's brewing. Most likely, the building won't burn down. There will still be deadlines to meet after lunch, clients to call back and reports to get done. However, if you can take at least a half hour of uninterrupted time outside and enjoy a healthy meal mindfully and intentionally, you might just come back to work refreshed, renewed and rejuvenated. Nature has a way of reorganizing your energy and bringing balance to your spirit.

4. During the day, take a moment from time to time to monitor two things: body language and body sensations.

First let's talk about body language. What is your body language saying when you interact with coworkers and clients? Does your posture indicate "I don't mind being approached" or are you on the defensive? Are you making eye contact or do you avoid looking at people when you talk to them? Are you on auto pilot or are you really listening to others and their concerns? Are you listening to understand another person's point of view or are you waiting for your turn to talk? Pay attention to your body language moment by moment as it can be a source of stress and can cause negative body sensations.

Now let's talk about body sensations. Pay attention to any stress or tension in your shoulders, face, back, etc. If you start feeling tension rise up—consciously let go of it by bringing your awareness to your breath and doing a quick body scan.

You can practice the Body Scan Meditation on page 36 in Part Two at any time. It doesn't always need to be a formal practice. Just bring your awareness to your breath on the intake and breathe into that part of your body that is holding stress with the out breath. Visualize the tension leaving your body. Breathe in. Breathe out. Short simple meditations throughout the day will give you a nice break to your day while relieving some of that stress that you are feeling.

5. Journaling.

One of the most effective ways to deal with difficult situations at work is to get your thoughts out on paper. If you are going through a stressful situation at work you know all too well that you will be replaying the situation over and over in your mind. What you said, what you should have said, what they said, how it should have played out, why did this happen and on it goes. There's a continuous loop that plays in your mind when you are distraught over something at work. Sometimes it even keeps you up at night. Instead of blowing up at work and having a meltdown, journal your thoughts. By journaling, you can release those negative and disruptive thoughts. It's a way to release your emotions and feelings without guilt or shame. It allows all those feelings to move through you, from your mind, to your arm, to your pen and out into the world. Here are a few tips when journaling:

- Make sure you write in a private space that is free from distractions so you can write whatever is on your mind with no limitations. Don't worry about being politically correct or whether you really would say these things out loud. Just grab your pen and go for it. No holding back, no stifling. Keep writing until you feel you've expressed everything that's on your mind.

- Give yourself time to reflect after writing. Sit back and read what you wrote. How does it feel to let it all out with no repercussions on whether you should or shouldn't have said this or that? Journaling can be very cathartic and helps us process difficult events and compose a coherent narrative about our experiences.

- Keep your journal private. Your journal is for you and you alone. When you keep this in mind, it can make you feel impossibly free to pour your authentic self onto the page. Imagine how this might impact your work life, helping you fully explore your emotions, release tension or aid you in shifting your perception.

Another core practice from the Mindfulness Based Stress Reduction program is the Mountain Meditation.[1]

During this meditation we practice becoming like—yes, you guessed it!—a mountain. We sit in stillness—like a mountain just sits there—unmoved by the changing of day into night, the changes of the weather and of the seasons. If you think about it, the mountain is always grounded, rooted into the earth, always still, always beautiful. It is beautiful just being what it is, seen or unseen, snow covered or green, rained on or engulfed in clouds. This image helps us remember our own strength as the seasons of our life change. Storms come and go in life and as the weather of our lives changes and becomes unbearable at times, we can still remain stable, balanced and grounded, like the mountain.

Mountain Meditation

This meditation is normally done in a sitting position, either on the floor or a chair, and begins by sensing into the support you have from the chair or the cushion, paying attention to the actual sensations of contact. Finding a position of stability and poise, upper body balanced over your hips and shoulders in a comfortable but alert posture, hands on your lap or your knees, arms hanging by their own weight, like heavy curtains, stable and relaxed.

Actually sensing into your body, feeling your feet … legs … hips … lower and upper body … arms … shoulders … neck … head …

And when you are ready, allowing your eyes to close, bringing awareness to breath, the actual physical sensations, feeling each breath as it comes in and goes out. Letting the breath be just as it is, without trying to change or regulate it in any way. Allowing it to flow easily and naturally, with its own rhythm and pace, knowing you are breathing perfectly well right now, nothing for you to do. Allowing the body to be still and sitting with a sense of dignity, a sense of resolve, a sense of being complete, whole, in this very moment, with your posture reflecting this sense of wholeness.

As you sit here, letting an image form in your mind's eye, of the most magnificent or beautiful mountain you know or have seen or can imagine, letting it gradually come into greater focus. Even if it doesn't come as a visual image, allowing the sense of this mountain and feeling its overall shape, its lofty peak or peaks high in the sky, the large base rooted in the bedrock of the earth's crust, its steep or gently sloping sides. Noticing how massive it is, how solid, how unmoving, how beautiful, whether from a far or up close.

Perhaps your mountain has snow blanketing its top and trees reaching down to the base, or rugged granite sides. There may be streams and waterfalls cascading down the slopes. There may be one peak or a series of peaks, or with meadows and high lakes. Observing it, noting its qualities and when you feel ready, seeing if you can bring the mountain into your own body sitting here so that your body and the mountain in your mind's eye become one so that as you sit here, you share in the massiveness and the stillness and majesty of the mountain, you become the mountain.

Grounded in the sitting posture, your head becomes the lofty peak, supported by the rest of the body and affording a panoramic view. Your shoulders and arms the sides of the mountain. Your buttocks and legs the solid base, rooted to your cushion or your chair, experiencing in your body a sense of uplift from deep within your pelvis and spine. With each breath, as you continue sitting, becoming a little more a breathing mountain, alive and vital, yet unwavering in your inner stillness, completely what you are, beyond words and thought, a centered, grounded, unmoving presence.

As you sit here, becoming aware of the fact that as the sun travels across the sky, the light and shadows and colors are changing virtually moment by moment in the mountain's stillness, and the surface teems with life and activity...streams, melting snow, waterfalls, plants and wildlife. As the mountain sits, seeing and feeling how night follows day and day follows night. The bright warming sun, followed by the cool night sky studded with stars, and the gradual dawning of a new day.

Through it all, the mountain just sits, experiencing change in each moment, constantly changing, yet always just being itself. It remains still as the seasons flow into one another and as the weather changes moment by moment and day by day, calmness abiding all change.

In summer, there is no snow on the mountain except perhaps for the very peaks or in crags shielded from direct sunlight. In the fall, the mountain may wear a coat of brilliant fire colors. In winter, a blanket of snow and ice.

In any season, it may find itself at times enshrouded in clouds or fog or pelted by freezing rain. People may come to see the mountain and comment on how beautiful it is or how it's not a good day to see the mountain, that it's too cloudy or rainy or foggy or dark.

None of this matters to the mountain, which remains at all times its essential self. Clouds may come and clouds may go, tourists may like it or not. The mountain's magnificence and beauty are not changed one bit by whether people see it or not, seen or unseen, in sun or clouds, broiling or frigid, day or night. It just sits, being itself. At times visited by violent storms, buffeted by snow and rain and winds of unthinkable magnitude.

Through it all, the mountain sits.

Spring comes, trees leaf out, flowers bloom in the high meadows and slopes, birds sing in the trees once again. Streams overflow with the waters of melting snow. Through it all, the mountain continues to sit, unmoved by the weather, by what happens on its surface, by the world of appearances, remaining its essential self, through the seasons, the changing weather, the activity ebbing and flowing on its surface.

In the same way, as we sit in meditation, we can learn to experience the mountain, we can embody the same central, unwavering stillness and groundedness in the face of everything that changes in our own lives; over seconds, over hours, over years. In our lives and in our meditation practice, we experience constantly the changing nature of mind and body and of the outer world, we have our own periods of light and darkness, activity and inactivity, our moments of color and our moments of drabness. It's true that we experience storms of varying intensity and violence in the outer world and in our own minds and bodies, buffeted by high winds, by cold and rain, we endure periods of darkness and pain, as well as the moments of joy and uplift, even our appearance changes constantly, experiencing a weather of its own.

By becoming the mountain in our meditation practice, we can link up with its strength and stability and adopt them for our own. We can use its energies to support our energy to encounter each moment with mindfulness and equanimity and clarity. It may help us to see that our thoughts and feelings, our preoccupations, our emotional storms and crises, even the things that happen to us are very much like the weather on the mountain. We tend to take it all personally, but its strongest characteristic is impersonal.

The weather of our own lives is not be ignored or denied, it is to be encountered, honored, felt, known for what it is, and held in awareness.

And in holding it in this way, we come to know a deeper silence and stillness and wisdom.

Mountains have this to teach us and much more if we can let it in.

So, if you find you resonate in some way with the strength and stability of the mountain in your sitting, it may be helpful to use it from time to time in your meditation practice, to remind you of what it means to sit mindfully with resolve and with wakefulness, in true stillness.

Notes

Notes

Part Four

The planet does not need more 'successful people'. The planet desperately needs more peacemakers, healers, restorers, storytellers and lovers of all kinds. It needs people to live well in their places. It needs people with moral courage willing to join the struggle to make the world habitable and humane and these qualities have little to do with success as our culture is the set.

—Dalai Lama

As the Dalai Lama so eloquently stated in the above quote, we need more peacemakers and healers in this world. The world doesn't lack this but it could definitely use more people aligned with these qualities. At the beginning of this quote, he addresses the notion of "successful people." We are so used to thinking of success and thus, successful people in the context of money, career promotions, and possibly the ability to maintain and keep relationships. For instance, if you're married, have kids and have a stable job with stature, you are deemed successful in many cultures. People who have done this are people that are perceived to have made all the "right" choices or for the pessimist, they are people that luck just "shines" on. They are people who are perceived to have followed all the rules by the book and have managed to meet or exceed some artificial criteria and standards in society—created by society—for success. Those that are outside of this box are deemed unsuccessful and are leading unsuccessful lives. How far from the truth that is.

We need to think about what true success is and redefine what "success" looks like by thinking about things that matter the most. Leaders in all professions can and do make a difference in people's lives. Leaders have the ability to influence their employees by motivating, inspiring and empowering them to become the best version of themselves and in that way can truly be considered "successful." This takes a certain kind of leadership trait, as well as someone who is not afraid to lead from their heart. It takes a person to step up, to become that leader that the Dalai Lama envisioned to help transform and re-envision the work environment into the place we hope for by bringing mindfulness to the workplace.

As mentioned in Part Three, every job has an element of stress to it. It doesn't matter where you work or what you do. However, when you are in a leadership position or a position where you have to lead by virtue of your role, you have an added level of stress. This stress sometimes comes in the form of what we call "people stress." One of the many challenges that leaders face is in helping to create and maintain a work environment that remains positive. A positive environment is conducive to a productive team.

According to Janice Marturano, blogger at Happify.com,[1] "Everyone has the capacity to lead with excellence. Leadership is not about fancy titles and heightened pay grades. At the heart of it, leadership is about influence. And this influence can really make a difference in people's lives. Each choice we make, each and every day, has an influence on our own life, as well as the lives of our family, friends, coworkers, employees, clients . . . for better or for worse." These aspects of our lives are all connected through us as an individual person. Everything we need to know is inside us. So the work of mindful leadership is to begin to see how we can train our mind and open ourselves up to the wisdom that lies within us.

I agree with Rob Dube, President and Cofounder of imageOne when he states "I view being a leader as a gift because it provides the unique opportunity to make a difference in the lives of others. I take the responsibility that comes with this gift very seriously and try to make the most it, constantly studying how to best utilize leadership skills to make a positive impact."[2] In the section below, we've adapted some of his suggestions for mindful leaders and added some items of our own.

Mindful Leaders

*M*indful leaders come to work ready to inspire and empower those around them. They are transformational in a sense. It is however sometimes difficult to lead with integrity, as there are constant distractions, disturbances and things that just "get in the way." From the moment you get to the office, you're bombarded with various distractions and tasks: Emails to respond to, reports to address, articles to read, employees to coach, clients to interact with, etc. It can be quite exhausting at times. So let's slow down and focus in order to make thoughtful decisions. Let's stay engaged with our employees to empower them, motivate them and help them excel in their careers.

Let's make a difference by establishing a consistent and formal practice of mindful leadership.

The Six Behaviors of a Mindful Leader

1. Your well-being is a priority.

Question for you: Do you come to work daily with an awakened and refreshed mind, body and spirit or do you start your workday exhausted and stressed when you walk in the door? Do you take time for breaks during the day to just breathe or do you plow through the day, sometimes not even taking lunch, leaving the office exhausted and ready to fall asleep on the couch at 6 p.m.? Are you aware of the old adage "You must fill yourself up so that you can give more to others?"

One way to do this is to set aside 10–15 minutes in the morning to meditate. Maintaining a meditation practice shouldn't be taken lightly and it requires effort. It also takes a good amount of discipline to meditate daily. However, the payoff is huge. You'll begin to worry less about day-to-day problems and focus on what is truly important.

As mentioned earlier, in this fast-paced, technology-driven world, mindfulness enables you to clear your mind of clutter and focus on what is most important. It allows you to make sound decisions that are well thought out and not reactionary. As our work lives have become filled with technology, the distractions we face increase immensely. With it, our ability to focus has diminished, but our need to think clearly in order to make safe and sound decisions has not. More than ever, leaders need to train themselves to be fully present, that is, to be in the present moment. This is difficult since so much of our lives, especially at work, require us to think ahead: the next sales quarter, projections, predictions, etc. That's where a consistent mindfulness practice comes into play, of which a formal practice of meditation will help tremendously and will help ground you. As you become more mindful, you will be a more effective, more successful and fulfilled leader.

2. You remain completely focused when people talk to you.

Question for you: During meetings, do you give your team your full attention? Do you really listen to your employees when they come to you for advice? Are you listening to understand or listening to reply? Our minds are going a mile a minute and sometimes it takes a great deal of effort to slow down, listen and remain present. Multitasking is viewed as a strength in most organizations. We sometimes forget we have a choice: Do we allow our minds to run amok, or do we learn to focus our attention on the task at hand?

One way to do this is to not only put your phone down but put it away completely. Really, put it away where you cannot see it or hear it. Most leaders are glued to their phone. That's where they conduct a lot of their business. Continuous conference calls, employees to call or text back, reports to read, emails, you name it. Our phones are our lifeline to our work sometimes. However, when you are having a face to face meeting with an employee or client, nothing says "You are not that important" than having a phone on the table in clear view. It unconsciously says "I'm talking to you, however, if that phone rings or vibrates, I have to answer it." Some people try turning the phone over. Sorry, not good enough. Have you ever tried to have a meaningful discussion with your boss while they are texting? Somehow it comes across as it's really not that meaningful to them. If you want to be an inspiring leader, put the phone away. Look into your employee's eyes and connect with them. Let them know you're invested in their growth in the company and really want to help them succeed. Such a simple act, however, it's truly transformational.

3. You empower your team members.

Question for you: How many times a day does a team member come to you with a concern or issue? As leaders, most of our days are filled with solving problems, putting out fires and just getting the job done so we can move on to our next challenge. I have news for you: A good leader doesn't just fix the problem, they allow their employees the time and space to reach their own conclusions, in their own time. Employees feel empowered when you take their ideas and thoughts about a situation into account. They feel trusted. They feel motivated. They feel inspired. Mindful leaders resist the urge to fix the problem and instead just give their employees exactly what they need: Their presence.

One way to do this is to stop telling employees the answer to their questions. The best way for anyone to learn is through self-discovery. So many times it is just easier and quicker to give someone the solution to a problem. We have the answer, we've done this better, we know best. I hate to break this to you, but that's not helping anyone. That's not empowering your employees. That's a quick fix that is not sustainable. Instead, let's try and help our employees come to their own conclusion by being a more collaborative leader. One that asks questions and remains silent while that person comes to their own conclusion. Remaining silent can be extremely difficult at times, however when we allow someone to work out their problems in their own time and at their own pace, it is much more empowering and also sustainable. Just be there for support. Be there with your heart, without trying to impose your will on them. This takes patience. This takes non-judgment. This takes trust. Having a consistent mindfulness practice will help create an atmosphere where you can pause first and allow presence to enter the moment. Empowering your team members is truly motivational and a sign of an exceptional leader. One that your employees will remember long after they leave the company.

4. You make thoughtful decisions and practice self-awareness.

Question for you: When you are at odds with an employee or client, do you take time to examine your attitude about the situation? Ask yourself: Am I more concerned with being right and winning the argument, or is it my priority to find a solution? Do I take time to make a thoughtful decision, one that is of the best interest of all? Do I have the employees' and clients' best interests in mind, the company's best interest in mind, or am I making a decision based on what's best for me?

One way to do this is to remember that we all have judgments. Most of the time our judgments are unconscious. Every decision we make involves an unconscious judgment, typically based on previous emotions or previous events. When we are able to pause and become aware of our own opinions about an impending decision, we can make a better conclusion: A conclusion that is in the best interest of all. Mindfulness will allow you to strengthen the awareness muscle in your brain, so you can manage your emotions, which in turn will help you make decisions without judgment. To do this, you must have a deep understanding of who you are. Mindful leaders are always learning and improving themselves. They are well aware of their strengths and opportunities and they take time daily to reflect on their decisions. This allows you to understand yourself better and know the areas in which you are strong and those that you need to work on. Being honest puts you in a position for improvement and growth, which can only lead to becoming more inspirational in nature. By making thoughtful decisions, you are enhancing the lives and careers of your team members, which is one of the greatest attributes of a mindful leader.

5. You start with caring and compassion.

Question for you: Do you take time during the day to talk to your employees and find out what's going on in their lives or do you keep personal conversations to a minimum? Do you have patience with your employees when they make a mistake or do you reprimand them and tell them what they "should" have done? Are you the kind of leader that employees are comfortable coming to for advice, or are you emotionally detached at work?

One way to do this is to check in with your employees daily. Make sure you take time to learn about your employees, their families and what's important to them. Every conversation at work doesn't have to be work-related. When you listen and learn about your employees' hopes and dreams, you become that inspirational leader. You become the boss that everyone wants to work for and in turn everyone will work tirelessly for. When you take time to get to know your employees on a personal level, it translates to "I hear you. I understand you. I want to help you succeed." Compassion starts with opening your heart to the feelings of others without judgment. Now compassion does not mean we overlook the mistakes made by our employees. It means we have sympathy and understanding of their difficulties and know we are not different from them. It starts with caring and compassion and requires a level of selflessness. This is truly what a mindful leader looks like. As Theodore Roosevelt once said, "Nobody cares how much you know until they know how much you care."

6. You are a servant leader.

Question for you: Is your main focus to move up the corporate ladder or do you focus on the needs of your employees? Do you make decisions with the team's best interest in mind, or is the decision based on your own agenda? Do you take responsibility for the actions and performances on your team or do you put blame on individuals before assessing whether you could be a better coach?

One way to do this is to have the awareness that your role as a leader is to serve others. Servant leadership involves putting your team first and yourself second. While the idea of servant leadership goes back at least two thousand years, the modern servant leadership movement was launched by Robert K. Greenleaf (1970) with the publication of his classic essay, "The Servant as Leader".[1] It was in that essay that he coined the words "servant-leader" and "servant leadership." Greenleaf defined the servant-leader as follows:

> *The servant-leader is servant first . . . It begins with the natural feeling that one wants to serve, to serve first. Then conscious choice brings one to aspire to lead. That person is sharply different from one who is leader first, perhaps because of the need to assuage an unusual power drive or to acquire material possessions... The leader-first and the servant-first are two extreme types. Between them, there are shadings and blends that are part of the infinite variety of human nature.*
>
> *The difference manifests itself in the care taken by the servant-first to make sure that other people's highest priority needs are being served. The best test, and difficult to administer, is: Do those served grow as persons? Do they, while being served, become healthier, wiser, freer, more autonomous, more likely themselves to become servants? And, what is the effect on the least privileged in society? Will they benefit or at least not be further deprived?*

Servant leaders help employees develop the skills they need to advance in their careers, even if it means moving up and out of their current position. How to become a servant leader? By consistently practicing the seven attitudes of mindfulness at work: Non-judging, trust, acceptance, patience, non-striving, beginner's mind, and letting go. When we bring these attitudes to work, we cultivate a new type of leadership. A leadership of presence. We develop self-awareness in order to inspire, motivate and empower our team with authenticity, vulnerably and compassion.

A sure way to incorporate these six behaviors into your leadership style and create a Firefly Culture is to practice another core meditation from the MBSR program called "Lovingkindness Meditation."[2] During the meditation, we practice giving compassion to ourselves, our loved ones, people at work that never give us grief, and then to team members who are a bit challenging. When we practice this meditation, we remember people aren't intentionally being unreasonable at times. We remember they're probably just reacting to a situation based on the knowledge they have. We remember . . . we are all one.

Lovingkindness Meditation

*T*his meditation can be done in any position, and begins by taking a moment to be aware of any thoughts or feelings you may be experiencing right now, acknowledging how things are for you right now. When you are ready, beginning to bring awareness to body: feeling your feet... legs... hips... lower and upper body... arms... shoulders... neck... head..., beginning to feel the movement of your breath, the actual sensations of breathing, reminding yourself that you are here, alive, whole.

When you're ready, you might bring to mind the image of a person who you know or you've known in your life to be loving and kind to you, someone who easily evokes feelings of warmth and love, it could be a spouse or partner, parent or family member, a mentor or close friend. Someone who has been good to you, helps you feel safe and whole, whose caring easily emanates from them to you. And if a person, past or present, doesn't come to mind, maybe someone you know to be inspirational may come, someone it is easy to imagine sending wishes of well-being to, wishing them well, and if it feels right, imagining saying to them:

May you be happy, healthy and whole, (picturing them receiving your wishes for them)

May you have love, warmth and affection,

May you be protected from harm and free from fear,

May you be alive, engaged and joyful,

May you experience inner peace and ease.

You may have your own words and wishes for them, so feel free to use words that resonate with you. Taking a few minutes now to feel how it is to wish these things for them, letting yourself have the sense of the wishes for well-being emanating from you to them, connecting you to them and noticing how it feels inside you, as you send these wishes of well-being to this person you love or care about.

When you are ready, seeing if you can imagine this person or figure wishing these very same things for you, knowing that they have your well-being in their heart, imagining them saying to you:

May you be happy, healthy and whole,

May you have love, warmth and affection in your life, (imagining them close to you, feeling their presence and unconditional love for you, as they say):

May you be protected from harm and free from fear,

May you be alive, engaged and joyful,

May you experience inner peace and ease.

Letting those feelings wash over you, feeling their unconditional love and caring for you, letting the feelings of love and safety grow in you, knowing there is nothing you have to do to deserve these feelings and wishes, that they are given freely, without condition. Seeing if you can connect to the meaning of these phrases even if you might not feel all the safety and warmth right now, knowing that is their wish for you, and now seeing if you can have these wishes for yourself, hearing yourself say to yourself:

May I be happy and healthy and loved,

May I be safe and protected,

May I be alive and free,

May I experience inner peace and ease.

You may have loved ones for whom it's also easy to have these wishes for, a child or family member or dear friend, or even a loved pet, and if it feels right, saying to them, in your own way and with your own words:

May you be happy and healthy and loved in your life,

May you be safe and protected, and not suffer,

May you be alive and joyful,

May you have inner peace and ease.

If it feels right, seeing if there are others in your life you can extend these good wishes to, a friend, a coworker, a neighbor, saying to yourself, to them:

May you be happy and healthy and loved in your life,

May you be safe and protected, free from harm,

May you be alive and joyful,

And may you have inner peace and ease.

It might even be possible to expand even further out, to acquaintances, people you know of but don't have a personal relationship with: the people you see around town, your neighbors, even people you don't have strong feelings about, like the salesperson who checks your groceries, saying to these people:

May you be happy and healthy and loved,

May you be safe and protected, free from suffering,

May you be alive, engaged and joyful,

And may you have inner peace and ease.

And even if the wishes aren't infused with the same warmth and love as they were with a loved one, seeing if you can extend the wish, without the expectation that it should make you or them feel in any particular way, connecting with what these wishes represent, keeping these people in your awareness as you send these good wishes:

Wishing for them to be healthy and whole,

Wishing for them to have aliveness and love in their lives,

And if you feel strong and secure, and you're comfortable with this, you might try extending these wishes to someone who's difficult for you right now, not necessarily the most difficult person in your life, just someone for whom there's been some sort of frustration or misunderstanding. In doing this, it might help to remember that, just like you, they want to be loved. And just like you, they want peace in their life. You could say to yourself:

Just like me, they want to feel happiness and joy,

Just like me, they want peace and ease,

And they want to be loved and to know their loved ones are safe and healthy,

And just like me, they are doing the best they can with what inner and outer resources they have.

And if this feels possible to you, silently saying to them:

May you feel peace and ease, (remembering that if this were really true for them, that they would certainly be easier to get along with)

May you have love and warmth in your life,

May you be happy, healthy and whole.

Even if this is difficult, there's value in noticing what it's like to extend the wish, recognizing that you are not condoning their actions, but seeing in them a human being with some of the same needs as you: to be loved, to be safe, to be at peace. And, if this is possible, remember the circle that began with yourself and the people you love the most, family and friends, extending the circle to include all the many people you don't know who may live far away, in other countries or cultures, saying:

May you be happy and healthy,

May you have peace and ease.

May you have love and warmth in your life.

You could even imagine extending these wishes to include the animals and plants, all life on our planet and beyond, including ourselves, saying:

May we all be happy and healthy,

May we all be safe and protected,

May we all live together in peace, ease and happiness.

And now, as this loving-kindness meditation comes to an end, taking time to appreciate and feel what's been generated through this practice. And even if there have been difficult parts of this practice, knowing that this practice has the potential to increase your sense of aliveness, of connection and of belonging.

And when you are ready, letting yourself feel again your physical presence, sensations of your body, feet, seat, upper torso, neck and head, beginning to notice the movement of your own breath, bringing aliveness and nourishment to your body as a whole, just as your wishes of good will bring aliveness and nourishment to those around you.

Conclusion

*A*T OUR CORE, we are all mentors or leaders. Someone, some- where, is looking to you for advice or council. The key to effective leadership is the ability to integrate your head with your heart. If practiced properly, you will lead with excellence, integrity, and inspiration. In the workplace though, it's ingrained in us to be logical and to hide our emotions. The mind is held in higher regard than the heart. However, our hearts are where essential leadership qualities lie; qualities such as empathy, courage, and compassion.

Empathy allows us to be in another person's shoes and understand people better.

Courage allows us to act when needed and exert a strength and resilience.

Compassion is opening our hearts to the feelings of others without judgment. Now, compassion does not mean we overlook the mistakes made by others. It simply means we have empathy and understanding for their difficulties. By tapping into the power of our heart, we will discover our ability to be compassionate. At first, your ego will resist this. The ego will always bring up many reasons why someone doesn't deserve your compassion. It will also try and tell you you're are a weak leader if you lead from your heart (believe it or not, your ego will be relentless on this advice) However, if we can practice empathy, courage and compassion through our commitment to mindful meditations, we can truly be transformational leaders.

We are both extremely passionate about our mindfulness practice and incorporating mindfulness and meditation into the workplace. We've adopted these concepts and tools into our own lives and have seen a vast improvement not only in our work life, but our personal journey. Although nothing on the outside changes, we've become more grounded, fulfilled and at peace. We've tapped into that inner peace that so many of us are longing for. It all begins with mindfulness . . . at home, at work, as an employee, as a manager, as a supervisor, and as a leader. Truthfully, we have each consistently lead through love instead of fear and we will tell you this: Your heart will always lead you to a better outcome. And you know what? You'll be a fierce leader and one that's admired, loved, and respected. A leader who can create and connect with your coworkers and at the same time elevate each other and the world around you. A leader who is not afraid to show vulnerability, compassion and authenticity. A leader who believes they can change the world, right from their desks at work. Be that leader and create a *Firefly Culture, Illuminate Your Workplace by Tuning In to Mindfulness.*

So what's next? You heal. You grow. And you help others.

A Personal Message From the Authors

I'm extremely passionate about helping people bring mindfulness to the workplace. It's been a game changer for me. At home, I would read all these books on personal growth, self-help, and I started cultivating a better home life. However, when I went to work I became a different person. I threw everything I was learning away as I walked into work. When I crossed the threshold of my workplace, I changed into someone else because that's what I thought I was supposed to do. As I was climbing the corporate ladder, I would imitate people who lead from fear instead of from their heart. I used to be stressed out daily, every little setback causing me anxiety. Always anxious and fearful. That's no way to live, especially when you spend a good amount of your life at work.

I remember one occasion very vividly. My supervisor asked me to reprimand one of the employees by using fear tactics. She even said to me, "Make sure you make her cry!" Well, by the end of our conversation, someone was definitely crying. It was me. I went into the bathroom after that encounter and sobbed my eyes out, thinking I could never become a supervisor who intimidates others and leads this way. It was at that moment that I knew I would be a different leader.

Eventually, as I moved up the corporate ladder and became a manager, I allowed myself the freedom to do things differently and lead from my heart. In time, I realized I could bring all these beautiful practices that I was incorporating into my home life to my work life. And guess what? My sales goals were not only met, but exceeded. My new boss was happy. My employees were happy. My customers were happy. I was happy. The sense of contributing something, of creating, of helping others, of putting our knowledge and skills to work can help us feel like we are a part of something bigger. In my opinion, that's what changing the world is all about." —*Camille*

~

Meditation, and particularly the practice of mindfulness, has brought a sense of peace into my life. Incorporating mindfulness in simple ways to my everyday routine really benefited me greatly. For this reason, wherever I work, I always suggest my employees, students, co-workers, even bosses, to tune into mindfulness.

It is true that we live in stressful times and that our lives are very busy. Mindfulness brings the quiet and peace needed to think, focus, and ultimately succeed. As we have discussed in the book, the practices outlined can be used to reduce work life stress and ease any tension in the mind. These practices can be observed at home or even in the workplace!

There are many instances where I see leaders being anxious, scattered in their thinking, and obsessive. It is very difficult to work for such a leader; and, I hope this book can demonstrate what it means to be a mindful leader. In my life, I have seen first hand how practicing mindfulness has changed my own actions. It has taught me a lot about how to be patient, empathetic, and compassionate to myself and those around me.

—*Jasmine*

Notes

Notes

References/Notes

PREFACE

1. Killingsworth, M.A., Gilbert, D.T., Daniel T. (2010). A wondering mind is an unhappy mind. *Science Vol. 330*, Issue 6006, pp. 932 https://science. sciencemag.org/content/330/6006/932.full

PART ONE

1. Sitting Meditation retrieved from https://palousemindfulness.com/docs/ sittingmeditation_script.pdf. Script is used with permission from Palouse Mindfulness.

2. Additional Awareness of Breath meditation available at https:// camillesacco.com/meditations

PART TWO

1. Kabat-Zinn, J. (1990, 2013). *Full catastrophe living.* New York: Bantam Books.

2. Suzuki, S. (2011). *Zen mind, beginner's mind.* Boston, MA: Shambhala Publications, Inc.

3. Body Scan Meditation retrieved from https://palousemindfulness. com/meditations/bodyscan.html. Used with permission from Palouse Mindfulness. For more information about the Body Scan Meditation, visit The Palouse Mindfulness website: https://palousemindfulness.com.

PART THREE

1. Mountain Meditation retrieved from https://palousemindfulness. com/meditations/mountain.html. Used with permission from Palouse Mindfulness.

PART FOUR

1. https://www.happify.com/hd/what-it-takes-to-be-a-mindful-leader/

2. https://www.inc.com/entrepreneurs-organization/these-5-traits-distinguish-mindful-leaders-from-oblivious-bosses.html

3. Greenleaf, R. K. The servant leader. 1970.

4. Lovingkindness Meditation retrieved from https://palousemindfulness. com/meditations/lovingkindness.html and https://palousemindfulness. com/docs/lovingkindness-med.pdf used with permission from Palouse Mindfulness.

About Author Camille Sacco

Camille Sacco is an American Institute of Health Care Professionals certified Mindfulness Coach and Meditation Instructor and a graduate of the acclaimed Palouse Mindfulness Based Stress Reduction course. She is also the author of the book *Hippiebanker: Bringing Peace, Love and Spirituality to the Workplace.*

Camille leads classes and workshops on mindful meditations and her coaching sessions are infused with down-to-earth guidance. She is both informative and fun in her approach.

Camille explains, "I want my clients to feel comfortable so I create a learning atmosphere that is warm, relaxing and inviting. My goal is to help people tap into the wisdom of their soul by cultivating daily practices that will inspire confidence in the pursuit of living their lives with a higher purpose."

Camille also has a 20-year-long career as a banker and currently serves as a bank manager for a large financial institution. Over the course of her career as a banker, she has won numerous awards for profitability as well as for customer and employee experiences. She has opened four branch offices for her employer. She's proud to point out that her accomplishments and accolades are a direct result of her commitment to her practice of mindful leadership.

Visit Camille's website at www.camillesacco.com

About Author Jasmine Alam, Ph.D.

Jasmine Alam Ph.D. is a writer, educator and public speaker, who facilitates workshops on mindful leadership and mindfulness in the workplace. She is an Assistant Professor of Management, a member of the Social Policy Research Network in Canada, and has published several articles in the areas of leadership and management.

With ten years of experience in both academia and the private sector, Jasmine has won several awards for her research and teaching. She attributes much of her success to practicing mindfulness.

As a strong believer in the power of mindfulness, Jasmine is passionate about communicating how practicing mindfulness regularly can lead to a more positive and healthy lifestyle. She sums it up this way: "I think mindfulness is so powerful; for me, it's been a lifeline. Imagine how many people can benefit from this."

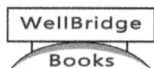

WellBridge
Books

WELLBRIDGE BOOKS
an imprint of Six Degrees Publishing Group
Portland · OR · USA

Bridges to Health & Wellness for the Whole Person Through Creative, Solution-Oriented Books

www.ingramcontent.com/pod-product-compliance
Lightning Source LLC
Chambersburg PA
CBHW030027290326
41934CB00005B/523

* 9 7 8 1 9 4 2 4 9 7 4 8 6 *